THE TRUMP
BOOK OF INSULTS

T0019526

A POST HILL PRESS BOOK

The Trump Book of Insults:
An Adult Coloring Book
© 2016 by M. G. Anthony
All Rights Reserved

ISBN: 978-1-68261-226-2

Cover elements provided by vecteezy.com

Post Hill Press
posthillpress.com

Printed in the United States of America

Major lightweight with no credibility

(On Politico Reporter Ben Schreckinger)

flunkie

(On CNN Contributor Ana Navarro)

Nasty guy with no heart

(On Evangelical Leader Russell Moore)

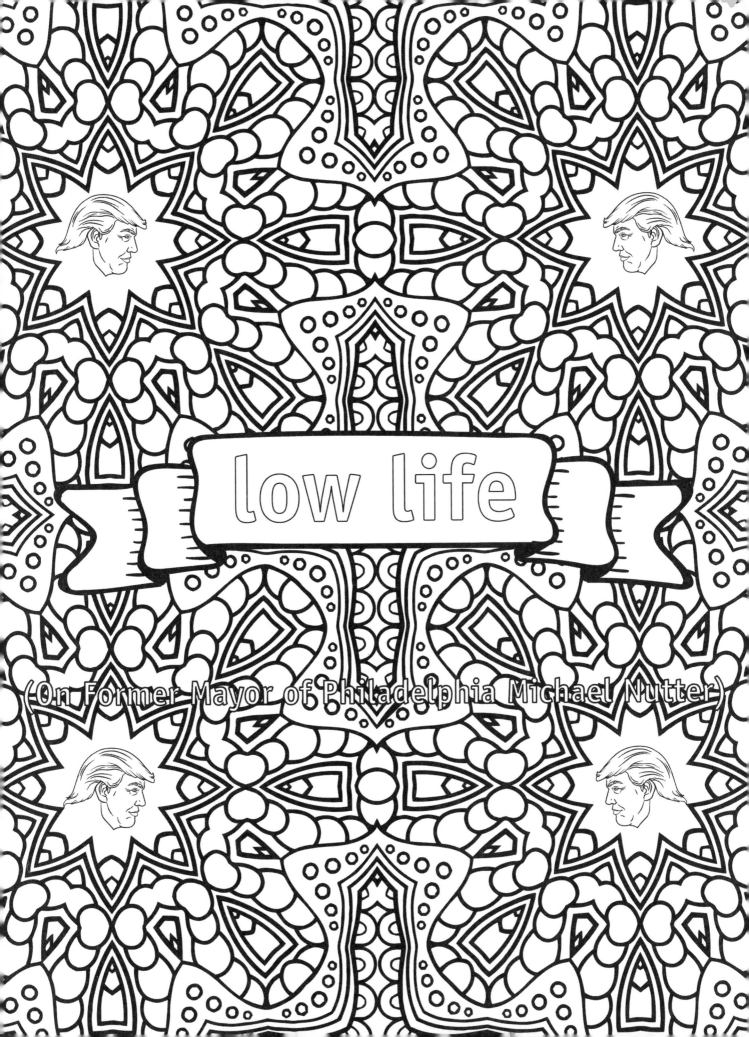

low life

(On Former Mayor of Philadelphia Michael Nutter)

MENTAL
BASKETCASE

(ON TALK SHOW HOST GLENN BECK)

Unbelievably nasty, mean enabler

(On Hillary Clinton)

Spoiled brat without a properly functioning brain

[On Senator Rand Paul]

Couldn't be elected
dog catcher

(On Former New York Governor George Pataki)

BORING, RAMBLING
AND
NON-SUBSTANTIVE

[ON PRESIDENT BARACK OBAMA'S
STATE OF THE UNION ADDRESS]

Wants to look cool, but it's far too late

(On Former Presidential Candidate Jeb Bush)

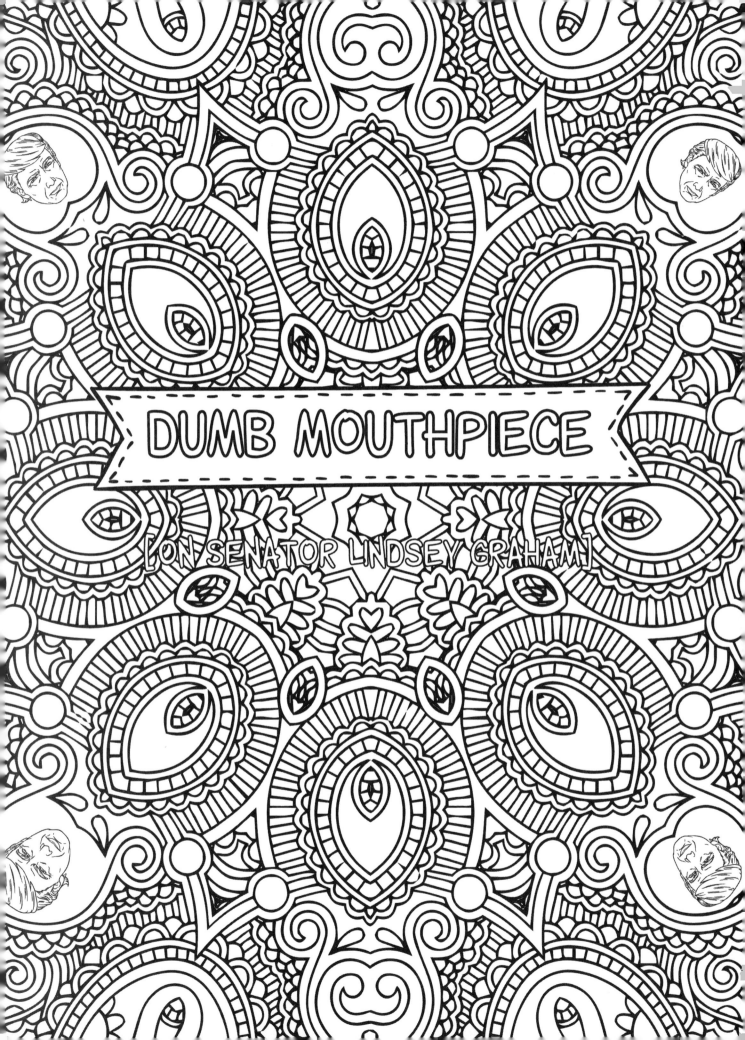

DUMB MOUTHPIECE

[ON SENATOR LINDSEY GRAHAM]

Total dud

On Ohio Governor John Kasich

Always seems to be crying

(On Talk Show Host Glenn Beck)

low class slob

(On Political Consultant Frank Luntz)

MAJOR SLEAZE AND BUFFOON

(ON CONSERVATIVE COMMENTATOR ERICK ERICKSON)

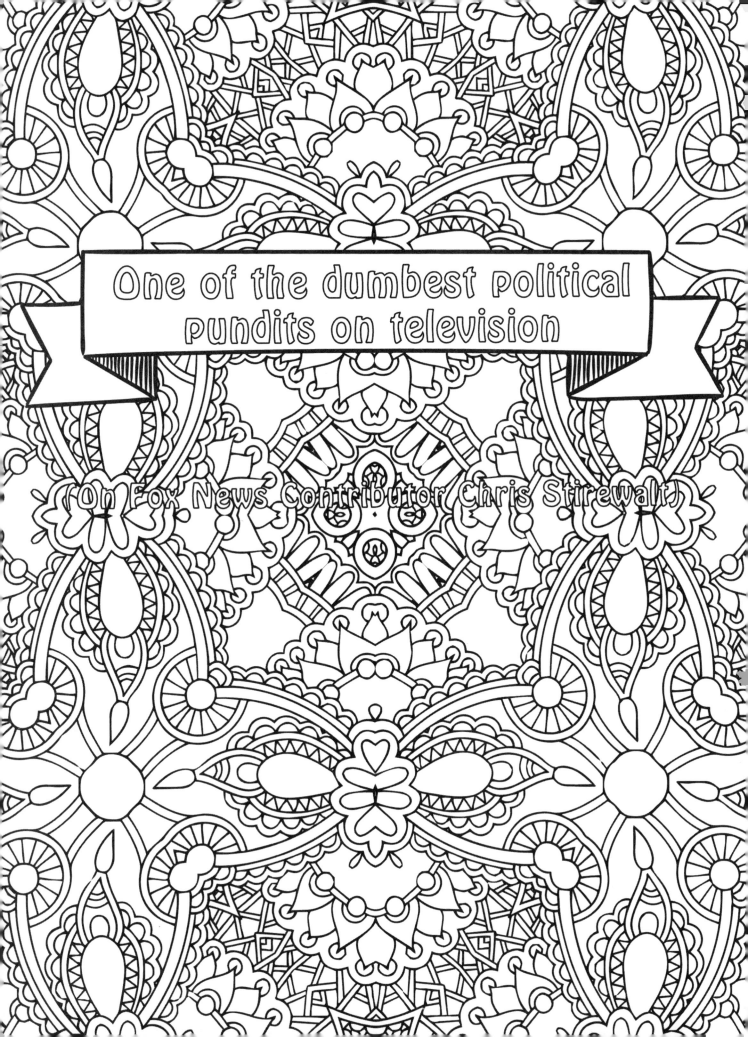

One of the dumbest political pundits on television

(On Fox News Contributor Chris Stirewalt)

Dummy

(On Former New Hampshire Governor John Sununu)

NOT ATHLETIC

(ON ACTOR SAMUEL L. JACKSON'S GOLF SWING)

A PENCHANT FOR SEXISM

(ON FORMER PRESIDENT BILL CLINTON)

RATINGS STARVED

(On Television Show Meet The Press)

looks more like a

gym rat than a

U.S. Senator

(On United States Senator Ben Sasse)

A dumb guy who fails @ virtually everything he touches

(On Political Consultant Stuart Stevens)

FIRED LIKE A
DOG!

(CNN POLITICAL ANALYST DAVID GREGORY)

Will NEVER Make America Great Again

(On Former Presidential Candidate Jeb Bush)

Also available from

M.G. ANTHONY

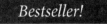

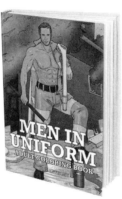

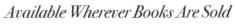